You're On Mute

Brimming with creative inspiration, how-to projects, and useful information to enrich your everyday life, Quarto Knows is a favourite destination for those pursuing their interests and passions. Visit our site and dig deeper with our books into your area of interest: Quarto Creates, Quarto Cooks, Quarto Homes, Quarto Lives, Quarto Drives, Quarto Explores, Quarto Gifts, or Quarto Kids.

First published in 2020 by Ivy Press,
an imprint of The Quarto Group.
The Old Brewery, 6 Blundell Street
London, N7 9BH,
United Kingdom
T (0)20 7700 6700
www.QuartoKnows.com

A catalogue record for this book is available from the British Library.

ISBN: 978-0-7112-6360-4
Ebook ISBN 978 0 7112-6361-1

10 9 8 7 6 5 4 3 2 1

Design by Eoghan O'Brien

Printed and bound by CPI Group (UK) Ltd, Croydon, CR0 4YY

Mute

101 Tips to Add Zip
to your Zoom

Jo Hoare

IVY PRESS

CONTENTS

INTRODUCTION

One day historians will look back on this period of communication and divide us into VC and BVC – video call and before video call. In 2019, Slack was something you asked your boss to cut you when you were 45 minutes late for the third day in a row, Hangouts was a code word for hook-ups and Zoom a weird ice cream from the 90s that a hundred nostalgia articles were written about on Buzzfeed. Sure, there was the odd Facetime call here and there, and, if you had family overseas, you will have mastered the awkward Skype call on Christmas Day. But by and large video calling tended not to trouble us too much.

Then along came the pandemic, bringing with it a whole wave of absolute awfulness that required us to totally change how we did, well, pretty much everything. With in-person meetings off the cards we flocked and fled to our screens with a varying amount of success. For every super-fun family quiz on Zoom, there was a mega-awkward four-way conversation on Houseparty. Although some experiences could be successfully recreated via a screen, lots could not. Love them or hate them, video calls are now here to stay, so why not make them a little easier on yourself? Read on for our ultimate 101 tips on nailing this now essential part of life.

CHAPTER

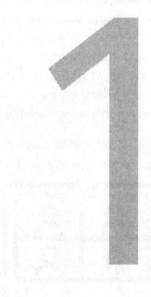

THE BASICS

Before we get into the nuances of advanced video-call etiquette, it's important to take time to understand the fundamentals. Get these right and you're well on your way to becoming a pro... Or at least not the person who at the start of every call takes 10 minutes to work out which way their camera faces or how to turn their mic on, while the rest of the callers roll their eyes and moan about you on WhatsApp.

THE BACKGROUND

"Thou shalt not judge," said no one on a video call, ever. Whether it's bored co-workers rating the cleanliness of your kitchen, "friends" you'd never actually invite round making snide remarks about the size of your apartment or your mother reprimanding you over your laundry pile, you can be sure that nothing goes undetected. Here are a few rules for an optimum video backdrop.

1.
KEEP IT CLEAN

With few of us lucky enough to have space for a dedicated office, chances are you'll be sat in a room used for other purposes, such as living, eating and sleeping. If so, do at least tidy up the 2 metres visible on screen. Anything outside that viewing zone? Do whatever you like.

2.
KEEP IT CLEAN PT 2

It goes without saying, any products of an intimate nature should be safely hidden in a cupboard. As should any partially clothed partners/roommates liable to walk into view.

3.
GO PRO

For work purposes, a plain-ish wall is ideal. Woe betide the person issuing out some sensitive news about falling profits with a "Live, Love, Laugh" decal over their right shoulder.

4.
DON'T BECOME A POTATO

Don't fake backgrounds. The ones you can choose on Zoom are as weird as hell. So is the sinister "blurred" option on Teams. Backgrounds don't make you look like you're in a cool coffee shop, perched on a hillside or floating in space. Instead, at best you resemble a poltergeist and at worst a person who's got something really, really suspicious behind them. Spare a thought for the boss who transformed herself into a potato, then spent the rest of the meeting trying to work out how to turn herself back again. Consider also the cautionary tale of the journalist interviewing an A-lister. The poor scribe left on a joke background of a popular meme featuring a family fighting over bathroom habits, leading the A-lister to believe it was their actual family. DISGUSTIN'!

5.
TRY A SPOT OF ZOOM-SCAPING

No, this isn't a new pubic hair trend, it's just placing your *objet d'art* and *objet du jour* (aka your fancy stuff) strategically so everyone can see you own Instagram's favourite vase/kept your cheese plant alive/nailed the curated gallery wall. Think of it like a 3-D Instagram flat lay and you're sorted.

6.
HEAVY PETTING

Don't panic about your pets. From the pug whose snoring interrupted a high-court judge's sentencing to the cat who jumped onto a laptop and gave hundreds of people on a webinar an extremely detailed view of its posterior, people mostly love a flash of a furry friend. At least it's a welcome change from Excel spreadsheets and budget reports.

7.
JUST KIDDING

And if the occasional kid comes spinning into the room demanding more snacks to keep quiet, that's fine, too. Just maybe make sure the in-call conversation is rated PG… "Daddy, what's inappropriate sexual conduct in the workplace?"

8.
BED HEAD

If you've got nowhere to sit in your make-shift workspace apart from your bed, then no one's judging that. But remember there's a big difference between ON and IN.

9.
LIGHTS, CAMERA, ACTION

If you're trying to impress and look your best on camera, then you want natural light diffused across your face. Sitting facing a window should achieve this, but if the look you're aiming for is more "taken into witness protection and can't have their identity revealed", then sit with a window behind you.

10.
WISH YOU WEREN'T HERE

Thanks to technology we know you can pick up your video call anywhere, but NEVER attempt to take one in the bathroom, OK?

ETIQUETTE

We had to learn a whole new set of rules when texting became the norm (who knew punctuation marks could be so insulting?), and in much the same way video calling requires us to get to grips with a fresh set of dos and don'ts. From the right way to say hello to knowing when to hang up, make sure you don't fall into poor videtiquette (yeah OK, despite best efforts I admit that phrase doesn't really work and won't catch on). Largely an issue pertaining to the office – because your family and friends already know you're rude – stick to the following etiquette advice and hopefully you won't make any work enemies… Or at least any new ones.

11.
DON'T SWEAT THE SMALL STUFF?

To small talk or not to small talk? In a friends and/ or family call you're not going to get out of it, unless you're *that* one in the group. On a work call it's trickier and a simple "Nice weekend?" can last longer than the actual weekend once 10 participants have had their go. A handy trick is to pass the buck and claim some people have mentioned they're on a very tight timeline, so you're going to "dive straight in". No one needs to know "some people" is actually you and the delicious sandwich you don't want to be kept apart from for a second longer than necessary.

12.
SOUND IT OUT

If you've got a computer from the same alumni year as the Enigma machine (which in the parlance of certain brands means you bought it 3 years ago and there's already been 14 updates), chances are the microphone and speakers aren't that great. A pair of headphones can help because they will reduce the dreaded nails-down-a-blackboard feedback screech.

13.
THE LONG GOODBYE

Hands up who else has been channelling kids' TV presenters and unleashing a "big wave" goodbye at the end of some really quite serious meetings. There's something a bit brutal about just hitting the "leave meeting" button, so we've unilaterally all decided it needs to be softened with a clownish rainbow-shaped wave. Adapt to a more laissez-faire single palm raise if that's more your style.

14.
MAKE A CONNECTION

Sure, your poor connection in weeks 1 to 4 of lockdown was OK. Cute even. You were frozen in time, robot voiced, dipping in and out like the 2020 version of a ghost and a ouija board. How we laughed. But now? Just upgrade your package, steal your neighbour's password or buy a dongle; everyone's had enough.

15.
DRESSED TO IMPRESS

So the stereotype is that working from home means wearing three-day-old PJs and having hair that was last washed back when blowing out candles on a birthday cake was still allowed. For a lot of us the stereotype rings true, but it's probably not going to win you that promotion any time soon. That being said, there's also something inherently suspicious about the person who appears in full make-up complete with a pro blow-dry and draft-excluder false eyelashes on an 8am video call. Instead, go for something in between, or at least pull a clean sweater over your egg-stained nightie, hey?

16.
ONE AT A TIME

Video calling has reduced us all to a never-ending linguistic version of the "too many co-workers in an overcrowded office kitchen" scenario – "Oops no, you go… Can I just… Sorry, no you finish." We can't help talking over one another. Judicious use of the mute button can help, but so can shutting the hell up occasionally. Try it.

17.
WHEN TO MUTE

Are you taking part in a webinar or lecture? Mute. Is your neighbour just starting to strim their lawn outside your window? Mute. Is your housemate or significant other prone to making up songs about how much they'd like a cup of coffee? Mute. Do you have nothing useful to contribute to the discussion, but like the sound of your own voice? MUTE! MUTE! MUTE!

18.
BEWARE THE EYE ROLL

It's easy to feel you have a layer of protection through a screen, but people can still see your facial expressions, even if you've totally zoned out. Practise a stock expression of mid-level interest – any more and you'll look murderously intense – and try to stick to it no matter how annoying Sue in accounts gets.

19.
MAY CONTAIN CONCENTRATE

Let's be honest, we all get distracted once Keith starts going on about pension policy changes, but you need to be smart about the fact that you're WhatsApping your co-workers with your phone on your lap. Pop a pen in your non-texting hand and voila, you'll look like you're taking notes, rather than denigrating Keith's wallpaper choices.

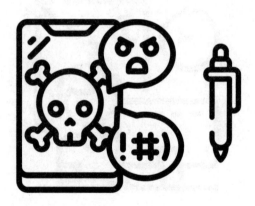

20.
GIVE PEOPLE A BREAK

Don't schedule in back-to-back video meetings.
It's highly unlikely your co-callers will have
a commode installed.

21.
FOOD FOR THOUGHT

If someone has broken the
above rule, you might be left
with no option but to eat on
the job. In that case try to
restrict your meal choices to non-messy foods and
never take a mouthful if there's any chance you'll
be required to talk. A sneaky cookie during a long
presentation is fine, but Diane in HR really doesn't
need to see you slurping up spaghetti at 11am.

CHAPTER

2

FRIENDS AND FAMILY

You'd be forgiven for thinking work would be the place where most of your video call issues would become apparent. That was until your whole family – including those who consider ATMs to be a bit new-fangled – got in on the act. At least at work you have an IT department to sort out tech issues; IRL you've only got yourself repeatedly shouting "YOU'RE ON MUTE, GRANDMA!" into the abyss. Can it be made better? Sure... Maybe. A big maybe.

22.
WHO'S THE IT GIRL? OR BOY?

Think of this like a designated driver. Someone in the family is going to have to step up and be the nominated tech support. Bribes may be necessary to make sure it isn't you. If it is, just tell anybody with issues to turn the computer off and on again. It's what the professionals do.

23.
MAKE A PLAN

OK, it sounds a bit ridiculous to have an "agenda". However, if you don't have a loose framework for your family gathering, then everyone will either talk over each other repeatedly or say nothing and descend into awkward "nice weather we're having" small talk.

24.
SIZE MATTERS

As intimate as a video call on your phone is (for more about that see our dating chapter on page 48), it's a lot easier for a group of people to interact and see each other properly on a bigger screen. Plus you won't get wrist ache (more on that in our dating section, too).

25.
DO GET CUT OFF

It's a good idea to have a planned end point to a family call. If, like 99.9% of users, you've been too tight to pay for Zoom's pro function and you get cut off after 40 minutes that can act as a good natural deadline. If you don't have a cut-off point in place, you may end up on the call until 1am watching your cousin strawpedo a bottle of prosecco and dissect her last four relationships.

26.
PATIENCE IS A VIRTUE

You might have spent 6 hours a day on video calls for the past 5 months, but remember not everyone has. This is new for some people and maybe a bit scary, so try not to be too cross when your cousin answers the call with a view of his ceiling for the 56th time. OK, he works in IT, maybe he's the exception. Give it to him with both barrels.

27.
MAKE IT SPECIAL

If the call is to celebrate someone's birthday or anniversary, think about what you can do to make it feel a bit less like the Thursday budget review meeting. Try something like a fun scavenger hunt, where everyone has to run away from their screens and come back with a themed object.

28.
INTRODUCE EVERYONE

If you're throwing yourself a virtual celebration, remember that not all of your friends might know each other or recognize each other via a screen when they only met each other once while wasted at your birthday several years ago. In real life people would form smaller groups and get to know each other, so you're going to have to make sure no one is left out.

29.
BAD NEWS TRAVELS

If you need to have a serious chat with someone about a subject you think they might find upsetting, then an old-fashioned phone call might be the better option. For example, dumping someone by video call is going to be painful for both parties. Nobody wants their new ex to be able to see their ugly cry face.

30.
BE KIND

You might be bored of video calls, but remember some of your friends and family might be feeling really lonely and this call might mean a lot to them.

31.
SET UP A GET OUT

If you know you're going to have to leave a family call early, then just let people know at the beginning. "My food shop is arriving at around 8" or "If the baby wakes up, I'll have to go" means you can do a quick dash with no drama.

32.
WHAT HAPPENS
ON THE VIDEO CALL...

This one is for anyone who has ever attended
a virtual hen party, stag do or bachelor party.
Remember that just because video calling has the
option to record conversations for posterity, doesn't
mean you should.

33.
IT'S NOT ALL ABOUT YOU

You might have loads of people around, but if you're
on a call to a friend who lives alone, try to give him
or her your undivided attention and take the call in
a room where you can chat one-to-one.

34.
DON'T BE LATE

If someone arrived at your house 10 minutes late you'd barely notice, but waiting for 10 minutes in front of a blank screen feels like an age. You're soon down a wormhole of paranoia, having convinced yourself that your friend is laying at the bottom of the stairs or has stood you up, when the reality is their internet is just being a bit rubbish. A quick text exchange will put your mind at rest. If you're the one who's late, try to let people know.

35.
JUST KIDDING

You know grandma wants to see the kids, but you also know they're going to get bored and fidgety after two minutes of chat, so try something interactive like the Zoom drawing game for a virtual bout of Pictionary. Failing that, tie them up. It's probably what they did back in granny's day.

36.
STORY TIME

Reading a story via video is super-cute for relatives who are missing kids, and it gives parents the chance to get half an hour to themselves to relax/ catch up on work/call a friend/down three large gin and tonics.

37.
GET OUTSIDE

If you and a friend are struggling to motivate yourselves to leave the house – aka you've sat on the couch for the last three days watching five seasons of *Below Deck* – then a shared virtual walk can be fun. Take time to show each other what you can see and you'll be surprised how much more interesting even your local park is through someone else's eyes. Sound like too much effort? Then tear open a giant bag of Doritos and crack on with Season 6.

38.
PLAN AHEAD

Got a special occasion to mark or a friend who needs cheering up? Order a takeout or Amazon Now delivery to arrive when you're on a call with the intended recipient. The doorbell going and a bottle of prosecco or box of brownies turning up will make them feel super-special, and you will get the warm fuzzy feeling of actually seeing them enjoy it. A word of warning: use this tip sparingly, otherwise when your birthday comes around you could end up with your bodyweight in Dominos dropping on the doorstep.

39.
JUST SAY NO

~~~~~~~~~~

Really don't feel like a video call tonight? It's OK to admit you've got VC burnout. Just reassure your friend or family member by rescheduling for another date and enjoy some "me time".

CHAPTER

QUIZZES

Never in the history of the world have quizzes been such a key part of our social life. Before coronavirus hit most of us took part in a quiz once a year, usually accidentally after turning up at the local bar, not having realized it was quiz night. Then lockdown kicked in and almost overnight you transformed into a bona-fide quizmaster, complete with gold sequin jacket and questionable dad jokes. But – and it's a big but – a quiz does take a bit of effort to run smoothly. Here's how to make your next family and friends video quiz an entertaining test of knowledge rather than a painful test of endurance.

40.
DON'T BE LAZY

Don't just rip off the first thing that comes up when you google "Zoom quiz," because chances are everyone's already heard those questions during the other 456 lockdown quizzes they've done.

41.
BEWARE THE CHEAT

Whether it's your friend's boyfriend who you never really trusted or your overly competitive cousin, someone's always going to try to cheat. Combat this by focusing on things that are harder to google. A section of music intros will do the trick, as will a picture round. Alternatively, use something like Google Forms, where you can create an online answer sheet and make everyone submit theirs at once. That way they don't have time to look at their phones.

42.
PERSONALIZE IT

Really want to impress your contestants? Write your own set of questions that all relate to the people taking part. If nothing else, you'll get to see a row between your smuggest couple friends when she realizes he has no idea what was the first song they danced to at their wedding.

43.
AGE OLD

If you're doing a family quiz, chances are your audience will span a pretty wide age range. In that case, making all the questions about TikTok dances is going to throw anyone over 25 (... a brief pause while we wait for older readers to come back from googling "TikTok dances"...) and all the kids will zone out with a music round that doesn't feature anything post-1990. Make sure there's something for everyone.

44.
SIZE MATTERS

Remember video calling can be tiring and will result in a shorter attention span than if you were quizzing over pints in the pub. To combat fatigue, keep the quiz short and sweet with around four or five rounds max. Any more than that and you'll notice a lot of "Zoom exits" – aka "the internet fakedown" when people lie about their connection to get away from question 43 of your dull medieval history round.

45.
TRUST A PRO

Can't be bothered to do a quiz yourself? We hear you. There are plenty of virtual quizzes hosted by pros that go out live online (try Jay's Virtual Pub Quiz, for example). You and your fellow quizzers can all watch at the same time and play along together.

DATING

Dating apps were pretty quick to get on the video call bandwagon, offering in-app calling and hints and tips for their users. However, for many of us the idea of sitting in front of a screen for 45 minutes asking your fellow dater if they have any brothers or sisters, while their internet connection buffers and you have a worrying feeling about what they are doing in their out-of-sight lap, didn't really appeal. Still, as we all got used to doing everything else in our lives on a screen and the prospect of meeting someone IRL became increasingly unlikely, a lot of us gave virtual dating a try. Soon we realized that maybe there were some advantages to getting a little video glimpse of your potential date, even when we could meet up for real.

46.
WORKING 9 TO 5

Remember you're on a date, not at work (unless you're sneaking one in on the company's time, in which case good for you). Relax, you don't need to be sat rigid at a desk and don't go into interview mode – this person is a potential partner, not your future boss.

47.
SURPRISE, SURPRISE

Making your date do a video call when he or she was expecting just audio is super unfair. You need to give the other person at least some notice and time to prepare. Plan a time for a VC that works for both of you.

48.
DON'T PUSH IT

If the other person doesn't seem keen on a video call, then respect their wishes. From a poor grip of tech to privacy worries or just plain shyness, there are heaps of reasons someone might not feel comfortable. You have permission to reassess the situation after several dates... Catfishing is real!

49.
SETTING
THE SCENE

Sure, taking a call at your kitchen table in front of the microwave and kettle, with a harsh fluorescent light overhead, is just fine for work. But for a call you hope might lead to romance, rather than redundancy, try to make the set-up a little cozier. AND BY COZY WE DON'T MEAN CALL FROM A SATIN-SHEETED BED LIKE A TOTAL CREEP. Some nice lighting, a comfortable spot on the sofa and no visible dirty laundry basket is a start.

50.
ANGLE FOR A SECOND DATE

Want your date to get a view right up your nostrils?
Presuming that's not your niche fetish (no kink
shaming here), raise up your laptop on a few books
so that it's level with your eyes; it will provide a far
more flattering viewpoint.

51.
STAY FOCUSED

Sure, it's fine to text during a dull meeting, but now
is not the time. And don't be catching up on *Selling
Sunset* in the background while your date talks. No
matter how boring they are.

52.
MANNERS MATTER

If you're not attracted to your date, don't use the "my internet dropped out" excuse to disappear. This is the video equivalent of climbing out of the bathroom window – and simply not cool.

53.
REMEMBER, REMEMBER

Before your call, cast a quick look over your date's profile, just as you would if you were worried about not recognizing them in a busy bar. You won't have the "Oh god there's four men in here with round glasses and brown hair" issue (unless he lives in a house with three other Harry Potter lookalikes), but it's good to remind yourself of some conversation starters from their profile.

54.
DRESS LIKE A DATE

Now no one's suggesting you go full bodycon dress or black tie, but a little bit of effort goes a long way. Also, spending time getting ready will put you in more of a date frame of mind than laying on the sofa in a dressing gown and wondering if the moth holes in your old sweater will be visible on camera.

55.
GET CUTE

Are you a couple of video dates into a new relationship or maybe doing the long-distance thing? There's plenty of creative ways to keep it fun online. Order each other a takeout delivery and have dinner "together" or set a challenge to "buy" each other a drink and both pick up the same wine.

56.
BODY LANGUAGE

Just as you'd lean in and look interested if this was a meet up IRL, try to emulate the real-date body language here. Not too close though – no one needs to be able to count your nostril hairs in HD.

57.
YOU'RE SO VAIN

We get the fact it's pretty distracting to have your own face right in front of you for the entire duration of a video call, especially when you're trying to impress. It's super-tempting to keep checking yourself out to see how your hair's looking, but try not to spend longer gazing at your face than you do your date. Appearing to possess a level of vanity that would make Simon Cowell consider you a bit self-obsessed won't go down well.

58.
DON'T BE A CREEP

Most people have come across someone inappropriate on a dating app and sadly a video call can take this up a notch. Just don't do it, OK. If that's really what you're after we hear the internet has plenty of pay- per-minute sites.

59.
GAME ON

The awkwardness of a first date can be supersized when you're both sat behind screens, so there's nothing wrong with a fun icebreaker. Try a silly game like virtual charades to loosen you both up. Just no throwing a tantrum when you lose. When your date realizes he or she is dealing with an 8-year-old trapped in an adult's body, there'll be only one two-word phrase on their mind: "hang up".

60.
MOVIE NIGHT

Wish you could take your date to the movies? Well, there's not much we can do to recreate the casual arm-round-the-back-of-the-seat move (unless you sit on your hand until it's numb and self-administer). Luckily all is not lost; you can watch something "together" by using a feature like Netflix Party, a Google Chrome extension (yes, we had to google what one of those is too), which synchronizes your viewing and has a chat function.

61.
STAY SAFE

Worried parent alert: please don't share any sensitive information. Even if you really, really get on and want to get it on, remember your call could be being recorded, so take some time to get to know and trust the person.

CHAPTER

5

WORK

With pretty much every office having to close once COVID kicked in, even total video-call refuseniks had to get familiar with the tech that would enable them to work at home. And once your boss, who never quite trusted you, cottoned on to the fact that video calls were the perfect way to make sure you were actually working, rather than sat on the beach idly answering the occasional email on your iPhone... Well, from that moment on you were never free of them. Basically, during the first few weeks of the pandemic if you didn't spend around 6 hours per working day on video calls, were you even in lockdown? But what about now? You may think you have got to grips with video calls, and don't recoil each time you're invited to join one, but as you will discover in this chapter there's still so much to learn.

62.
GET FAMILIAR

Make sure you know how to use the platform you've been invited on. Just like when you go to someone's house and have zero idea how to turn on their TV, all of the video-call suppliers have slightly different functions and woe betide if you're left out in the cold – or at least in the virtual waiting room – without a downloaded app/password/retina scan and facial recognition.

63.
EARLY BIRD

Unless your home office is very far away from your living quarters, the worst thing about video meetings is not being able to blame traffic or cancelled trains for your lack of promptness. The only valid excuses for tardiness we can think of are if you have extreme pandemic paranoia and spend all out-of-work hours isolating in a forest miles from civilization, or you're rich enough to have a private monorail between your home office complex and your mansion. In the latter case you probably own the company so relax, no one's going to tell you off for being 5 minutes late. For the rest of us, if a meeting reminder doesn't automatically appear in your calendar, be sure to set yourself an alarm for a few minutes before each scheduled call.

64.
CHECK, PLEASE

The temptation to log on for a 9am video call at 8.59am is strong, but if you've got a call first thing it's a good idea to check your internet or computer hasn't gone bump in the night. That way you've got time to tell people you're having issues. How you might do that if your laptop's busted and/or you can't access the Wi-Fi we're not sure, but it's the thought that counts. Heaven forbid you might have to pick up the phone and call someone... Millennials and younger, we're looking at you.

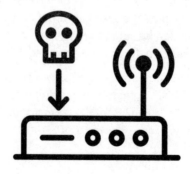

65.
MUST YOU?

Consider this: does the issue at hand REALLY need a video call? Do you need to send out a Teams invite to ask someone if they've received an email? You may have taken the death of your computer's mouse badly, but do you really have to inform the IT guy about its demise face to face? Would an email do the job equally well, if not better? VC fatigue is a real thing – overdo it and you'll risk being the girl or boy who cried wolf. Pretty soon no one will turn up even when you really need them.

66.
TRICKS OF THE TRADE

Good news lazy people. Most platforms have some in-built functions made to make your working life easier. Can't be bothered to take notes for someone not in the meeting? Zoom can record any meeting, even midway through (Alt + R, FYI).

67.
SILENCE, PLEASE

If it's a video call featuring more than three people, then stay on mute when you're not talking. Repeat: stay on mute. Not clear enough for you? STAY ON MUTE! Even tiny amounts of background noise, like shuffling papers or washing machines, can add up to a whole lot of annoyance for everyone.

68.
MEETING OR WEBINAR?

Got a big presentation to go through? Everyone chipping in constantly means you'll be here until the next pandemic hits, so ask to start the meeting with everyone muted and politely explain why. Politeness not your scene? Then why not adopt the manner of a Victorian schoolmaster and start the meeting with a theatrical shout of "SILENCE," followed by threats of punishments for any insolence.

69.
PICK CAREFULLY

In an office, most people don't mind popping along for a quick meeting. After all, it's 10 minutes away from your desk and you might even get some free sandwiches. However, video meetings can rapidly feel like they fill a whole day, leaving no time to actually get work done. So try to only invite people who are really essential. Does your boss, accounts guy, HR person, CEO and facilities manager need to attend a call dealing with your concerns about a lack of sandwich options now the all-day sales conference has gone online?

70.
BE SENSITIVE

Not everyone feels confident on camera and there might be a million reasons why someone prefers to stay audio only. Sure, one of them might be that they haven't brushed their hair for three days, but video calls also might make them anxious, their internet might be slow, they might be having to take the call in a room they don't want everyone to see etc. Make sure to ask if people feel comfortable.

71.
GET SOCIAL

Video calls can be a nice way of keeping your team sociable when working remotely. Raise a glass for the upcoming weekend with a 4pm fizz hour every Friday or set up an early morning coffee break where co-workers can drop in for a chat. The best thing about these virtual socials is it's now almost impossible to get cornered by Dennis in design showing you videos of his pets again.

72.
HELPING HAND

Sick to death of looking at yourself for all of
your working day? Some apps have a "touch up"
function; Zoom's gives you a flattering hint of blur
and smooth like a lo-fi Instagram filter. This feature
is made for mornings when you only woke up
5 minutes before a call.

73.
EXIT HERE

Saying goodbye on a video meeting can really drag.
This awkward moment can be the work equivalent
of those annoying couples who "argue" about who's
going to hang up first. Very few of us want to be
the person who just presses "LEAVE MEETING" the
instant things wrap up, and with nowhere to go it's
tricky to make a hasty retreat. A simple question like
"Does anyone need anything else?" works or, failing
that, clutch your stomach and run for the bathroom.
Nobody's going to ask about that…

74.
DON'T BE A ZOOM BORE

〜〜〜〜〜〜

It's harder to concentrate for a loooonnngggg time on one speaker on screen than it is in person. In no time your mind can idly wander to how many apples Ben's eaten or what the stain on Pete's tie might be (and why is Pete still wearing a tie at home?), so take care to be succinct.

75.
SHOW UP, DON'T SHOW OFF

If co-workers need help with their tech during a call, try not to be patronizing or impatient. Rolling your eyes and tutting as someone struggles to screen-share is downright mean, as is ostentatious use of advanced functions in an unnecessary way. Just be nice, OK?

76.
PLAY IT DOWN

~~~~~~~~~

Sure, you might have an absolutely gorgeous home and enjoy taking your calls in a different luxurious location every day, but remember not everyone you work with will be in the same boat. Keeping backgrounds discreet will avoid too much ill-feeling.

77.
STAY INSIDE

~~~~~~~~~

Tempting as it is to top up your tan while you chat, outdoor video calls are by and large a pain for everyone else who struggles to hear or see you properly. It does also smack of skiving. You could take a work call to discuss how a co-worker's ongoing neck problem means she's unable to move it and thus unable to work, only to see a wasp landing on her shoulder leads to a miraculous recovery… Busted!

78.
TURN ON, TURN OFF

Do you need to get up for a bathroom break during a call or have to walk across the room to get a drink/charger/pillow to smother yourself if you have to sit through another hour of this? If so, turn your camera AND your audio off. People moving around is distracting to everyone else and no one wants to be the guy who everyone heard pee.

79.
SPLASH OUT

Pay for the pro version of Zoom (and claim it back on expenses obviously). Nothing says amateur like having to re-log back in every 40 minutes because no one's upgraded.

80.
DON'T STAND SO CLOSE

If your co-workers can see your pores on screen, you need to shift your chair back a bit.

81.
SET
BOUNDARIES

Just because you can do a video call at any time, doesn't mean you should. Be respectful that people still have a life and need downtime. Don't be the idiot who arranges repeated 8am meetings for no reason. Saying, "But we'd be commuting then!" doesn't cut it.

82.
GIVE IT YOUR BEST SHOT

Remember when we were all getting to grips with video calls and the most popular posts on Instagram were fuzzy screenshots of you and your caught-unawares co-workers mid-meeting? We get it, things were boring back then. However, not everyone wants a picture of them with mouth open, eyes closed, looking gormless on your socials and you could even accidentally show something you shouldn't. If you want to take a screenshot for any reason, then ask permission and tell everyone in the meeting where it'll go. If you don't, you may find co-workers enact their revenge by posting those pics from you hammered at last year's Christmas party.

83.
GESTURES MATTER

We've discussed the "big wave" in Tip 13, but if you're on mute while one co-worker is speaking it's nice to show them some appreciation so they know they're on the right track. A big smile, interested nod or a thumbs-up will let them know they're doing OK.

84.
CHECK YOUR SETTINGS

If you normally have your screen turned up to
Chernobyl-reactor-explosion levels of brightness,
it's probably time to take it down a notch. A glowing
screen will give off a distracting glare, especially if
you wear glasses, which will turn into laser-beam
shooting eyeballs if you're not careful.

85.
MORE
IS MORE

If you're in a job where you need or want to wear make-up (or you have a major office crush), then remember video calls will bleach you out and dull definition, so a swish more blush and an extra coat or two of mascara are in order.

86.
GIVE PEOPLE WARNING

An unscheduled video call from a boss (or even just someone in your office that's hard work) strikes fear into every heart and is about as welcome as a fart in a crowded office elevator. Even if you need to speak to someone last minute, a quick Slack message or email telling them you'll call in 5 minutes and what the call is about will save their blood pressure.

87.
TRY TO BE ON A PROPER SCREEN

For emergency conversations your iPhone is fine, but for scheduled meetings that tell-tale selfie mode smacks of being unprepared. Whatever you do, never consider making a call before you've got dressed for the day – we've all seen those viral videos do the rounds on WhatsApp.

88.
BE HUMAN

~~~~~

If co-workers live alone (or with people they don't like), your face might be the only one they've seen today. Take a few minutes to chat if you sense they need to. Kindness pays.

JOB INTERVIEWS

Whereas a Slack chat or Teams meeting with your existing co-workers means you have some sense of what they're like, a virtual interview is a completely different kind of work call. It's a step entirely into the unknown and with it being harder to pick up non-verbal clues like body language on a screen, it can be difficult to build a rapport. Still, all is not lost. At least you can keep your PJ pants on under your desk, hey? (Don't do this, because no doubt you'll realize you need to walk across the room and get your charger halfway through and those unicorn PJs you've had since college won't exactly scream professional.)

89.
TRIAL RUN

Get a friend or family member to call you on the same platform the interview is scheduled on a few days before. That way you can check you know how to use it properly. Don't tell them when the interview actually is, otherwise they might find it hilarious to prank call in the minutes leading up to the actual meeting.

90.
DON'T BE A SLOUCH

If possible, take the calling sitting on a proper chair at a desk or table, and think about how you're positioned. Slouched on an armchair or sofa and you'll look way too casual for anything other than a model in the IKEA catalogue.

91.
WATCH OUT FOR YOUR OUTFIT

Remember that if someone can only see you from the chest up, an item of clothing that looks perfectly professional IRL might not appear the same way on screen. A shirt that looks fine when you can see the whole thing might come across as super low-cut on a video call.

92.
GO NEUTRAL

On other types of calls, a bit of personality can be cool but in an interview you want them to concentrate on you, not whether the monstera plant behind you is real or plastic. To avoid this, choose the plainest wall you can.

93.
THE EYES HAVE IT

Eye contact is crucial in an interview situation (though don't freak your future employer out by turning it into a staring contest). You might need to change the position of your laptop so you're looking straight ahead, like you would in a conversation. Balance it on a few books or stand up and put it on a shelf if necessary.

94.
CHEAT SHEETS

~~~~~~~~~~

An advantage of video calls is that you can have a few notes of prepared questions or prompts to hand, but try not to keep looking down the whole time like you're reading from a script. They'll clock your bald patch for a start.

6

THE PITFALLS

No matter who your video call is with, there are some drawbacks and hazards universal to all. From the serious matter of security to the shame of surprise screen sharing, in our final round of advice we're covering the definite "must not dos" in this brave new world.

95.
SOMEONE CALL SECURITY

Lockdown has given us a whole new vocabulary. What would you have thought Zoombombing meant this time last year? A particularly obnoxious way of entering a swimming pool at speed? Nope, it means hacking into other people's video calls. Reasons for this range from old-fashioned pathetic trolling to cybercrime, so make sure you use a video-call service that uses a password or waiting rooms.

96.
UNWANTED ATTENTION

Have internet, will perv. Anything online runs the risk of a load of deviants turning up and spoiling it for everyone. Take the... ahem... "gentleman" who kept showing up to a very lovely lady instructor's yoga class, but then seemed to mistake yoga for what we'll politely term self-abuse. If you're running a webinar or online course, be extra vigilant for this with your security.

97.
SAY MY NAME

Who used the laptop before you? Your mischievous nephew? Your Tinder-obsessed flatmate? Make sure you haven't been logged in as Professor Poohead or BigBoi4U.

98.
REFLECT ON THIS

You think you've got your background sorted: posh candle in view, fresh flowers, no mess. What did you forget? Aha! It's that mirror currently giving the whole marketing department an excellent view of your partner vigorously towelling off their buttocks. Beware reflective surfaces.

99.
SHARE AND SHARE ALIKE

Want to know the scariest question you can hear on a video call? "Can you just share your screen please." If you're not properly prepared, the whole call will at best see you've wasted the whole morning googling how many times it's normal to poop in a day and at worst five applications for other jobs.

100.
OTHER PEOPLE

As touched on earlier, the occasional cute kids or pets crashing a call are fine, but adult people, that's another matter. Hovering parents who just want to "pop in and say hi" to your "office friends" when you're in the middle of a work disciplinary are not OK.

101.
CHATTERBOXING

BE WARY OF IN-GROUP CHAT FUNCTIONS!
This is the modern day "I didn't realize you were in
the cubicle" scenario; the getting busted for bad-
mouthing a co-worker behind their back dilemma.
It only takes one case of mistaken identity between
all "group" and "private" messages and everyone
knows you think Brian in marketing is doing it with
the receptionist and your new manager's haircut
makes her look like a mangy German Shepherd.

ACKNOWLEDGEMENTS

To all my colleagues, whose stories I may or may not have pinched for this book and who have to put up with retina-detaching eye rolls daily.

PICTURE CREDITS

All illustrations sourced from www.flaticon.com.